Sweetest Mandalas Coloring Book
For kids and beginner

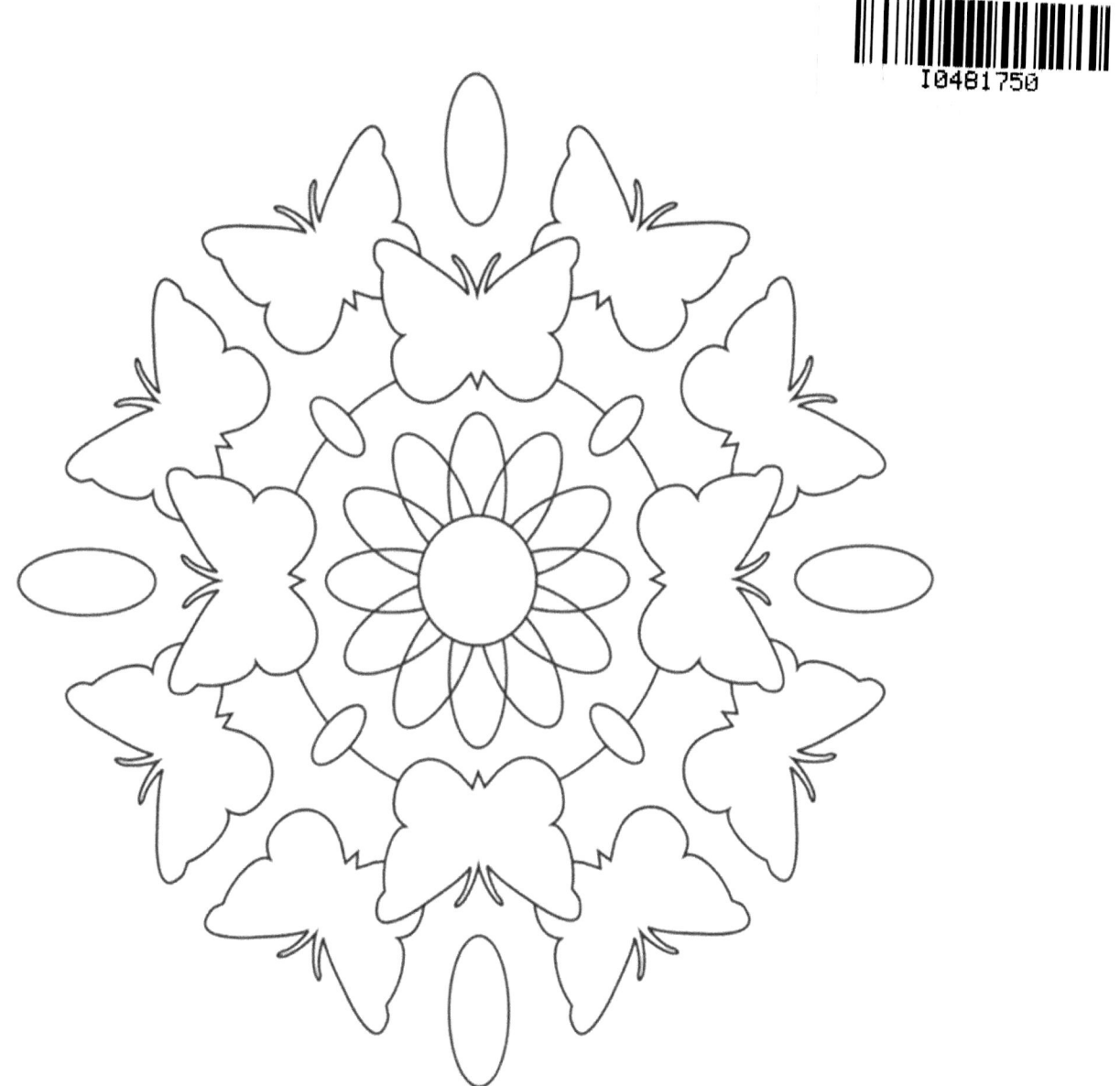

Nina Packer

Sweetest Mandalas Coloring Book
For kids and beginner

ISBN-13: 978-1983954757

ISBN-10: 1983954756

ISBN-13: 978-1983956218

ISBN-10: 198395621X

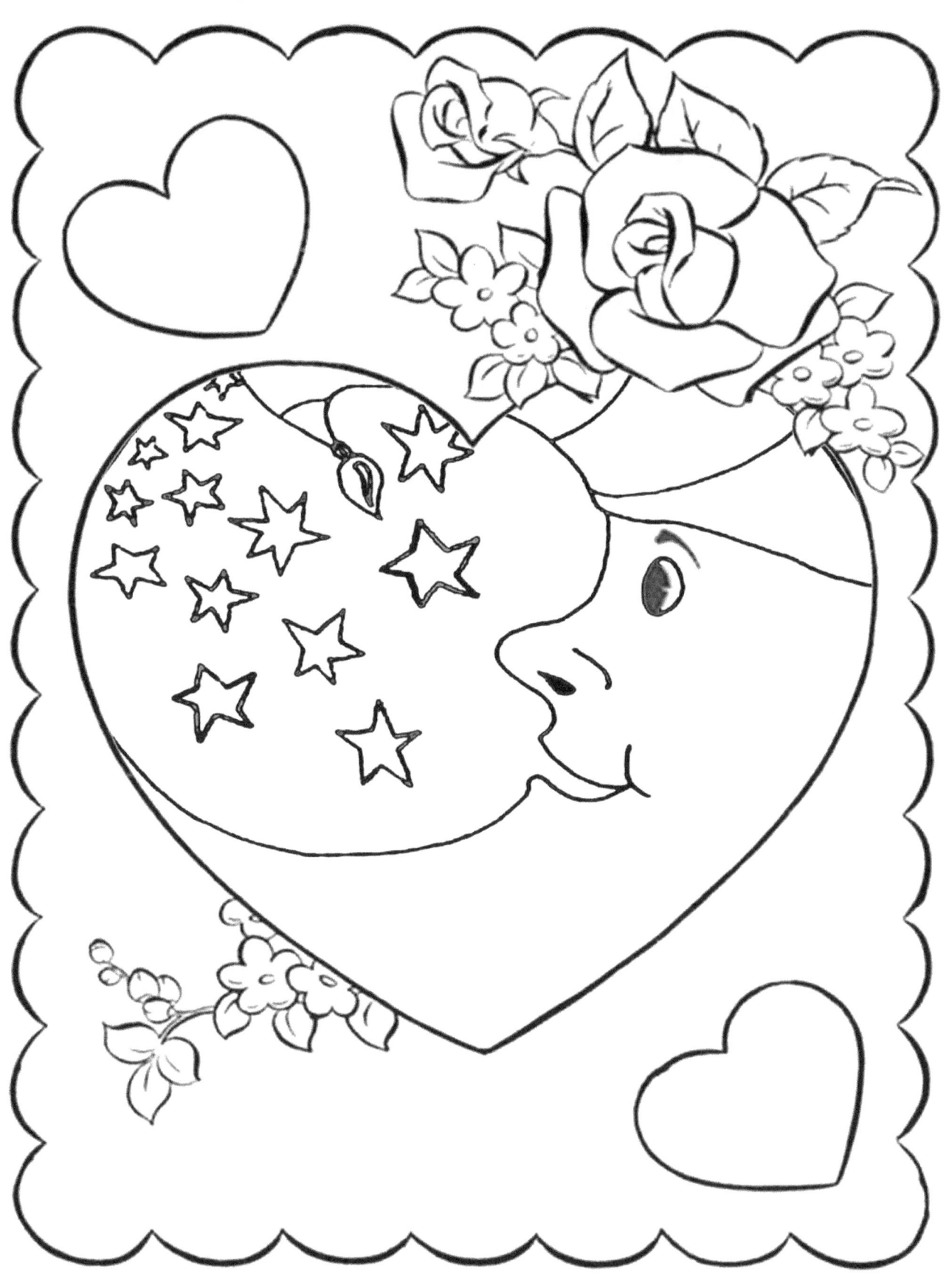

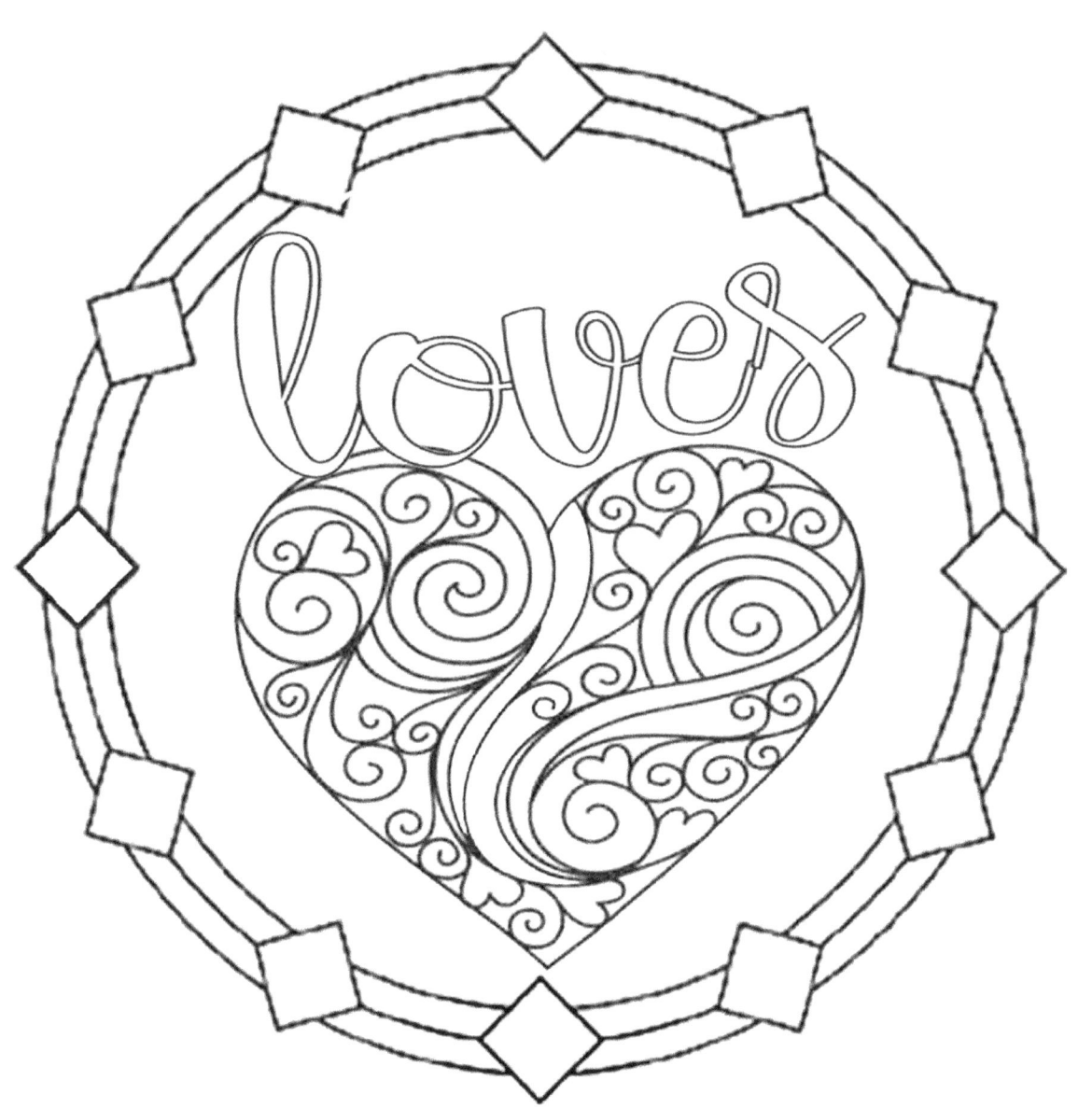

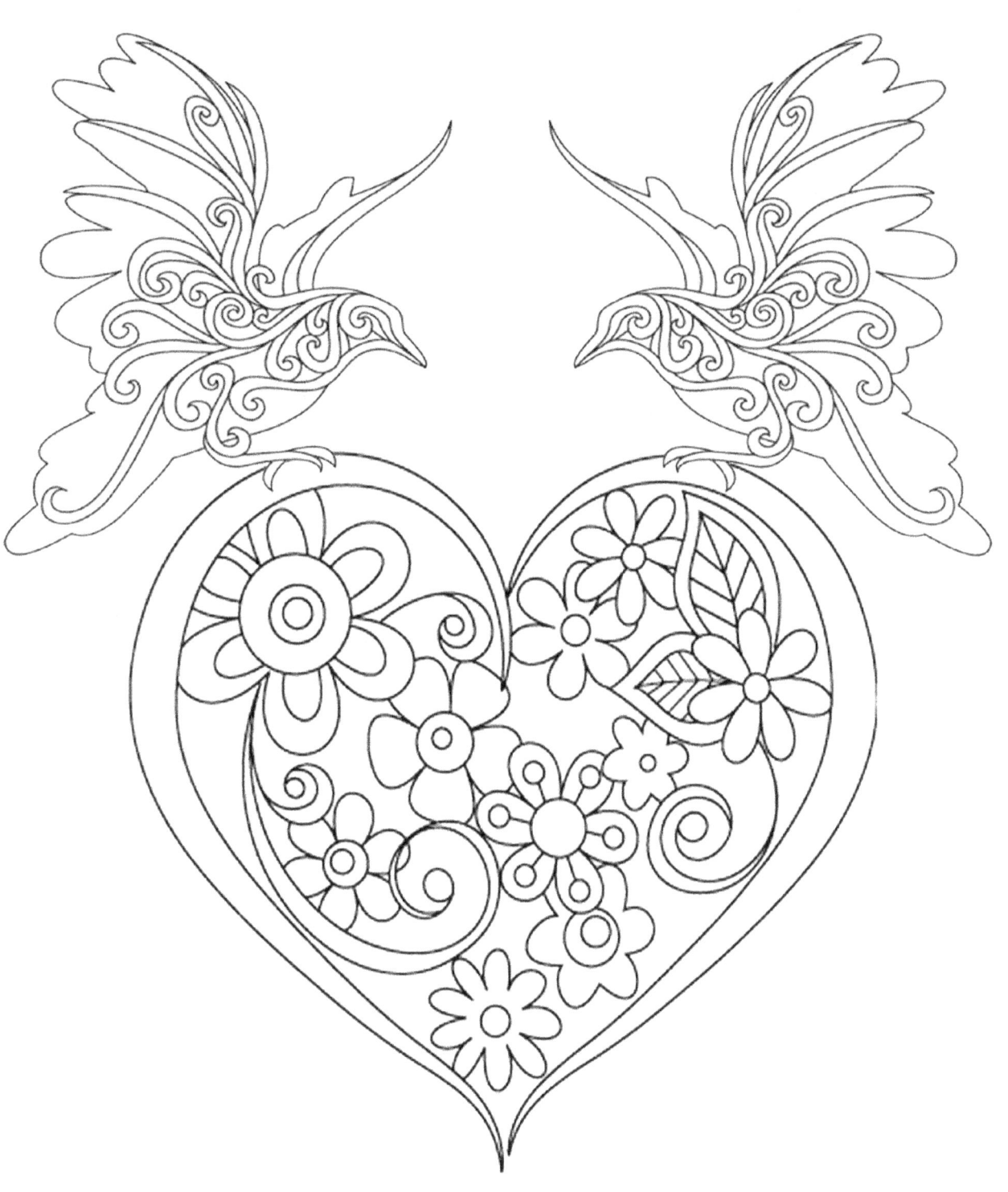

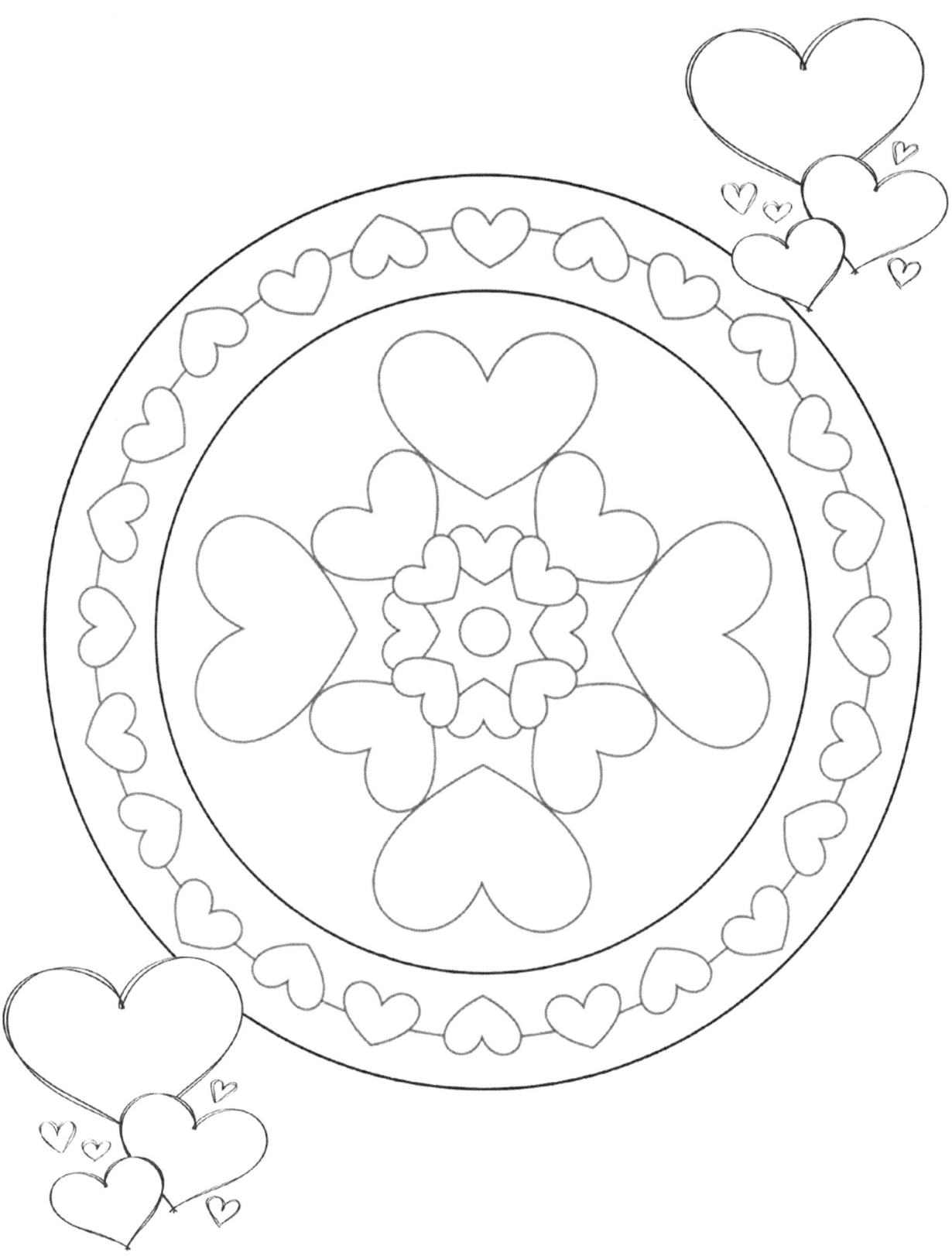

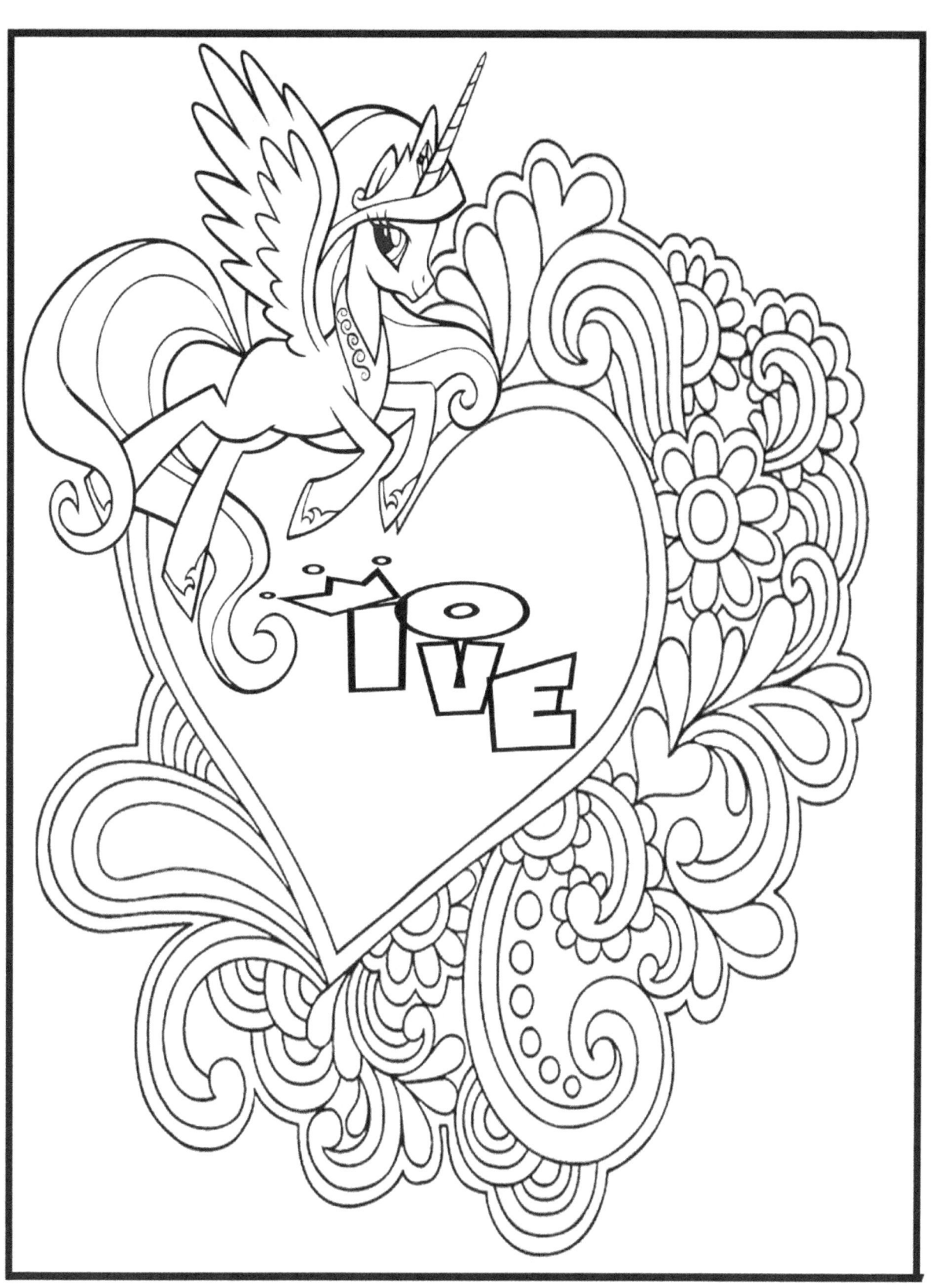

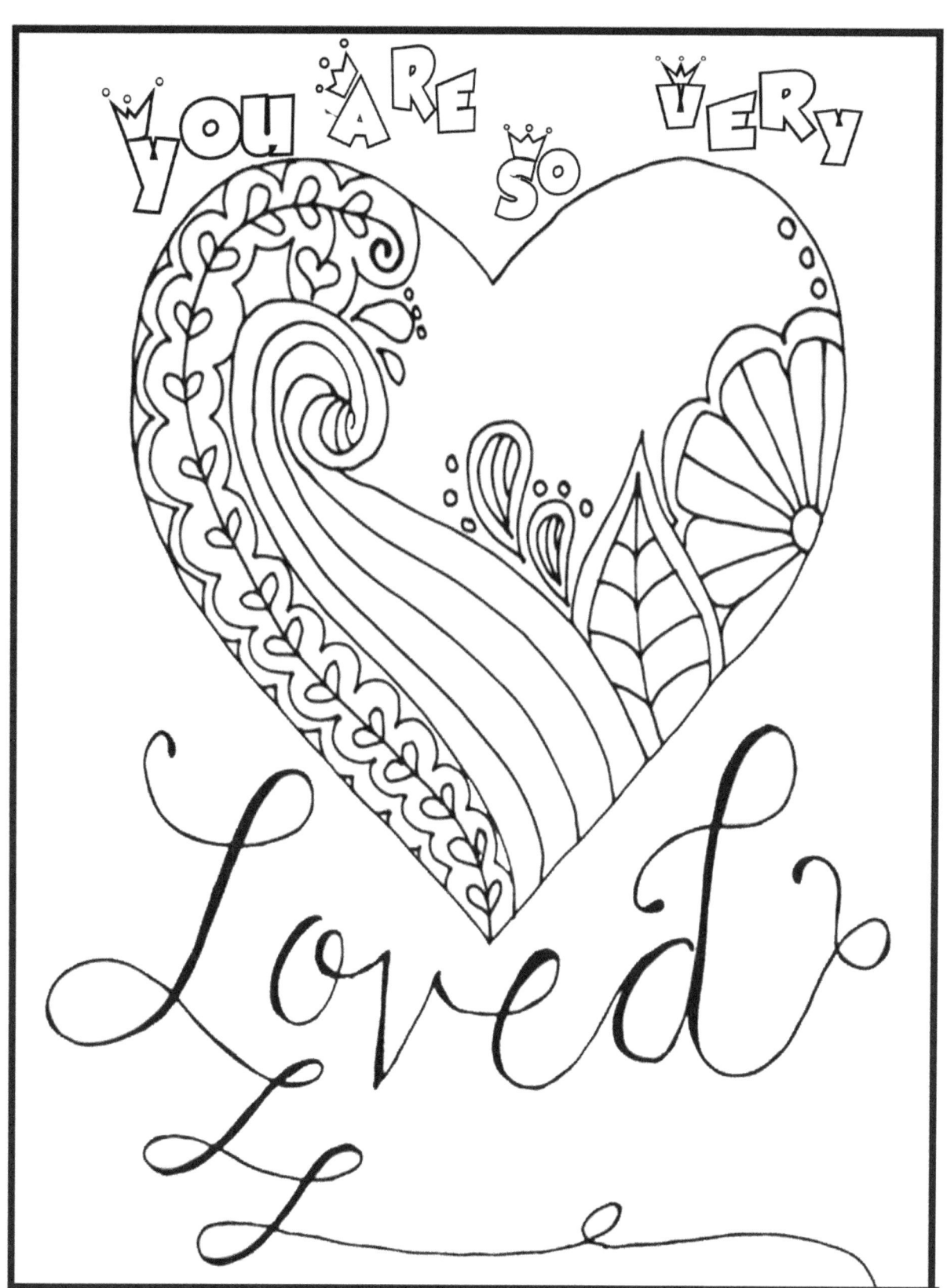

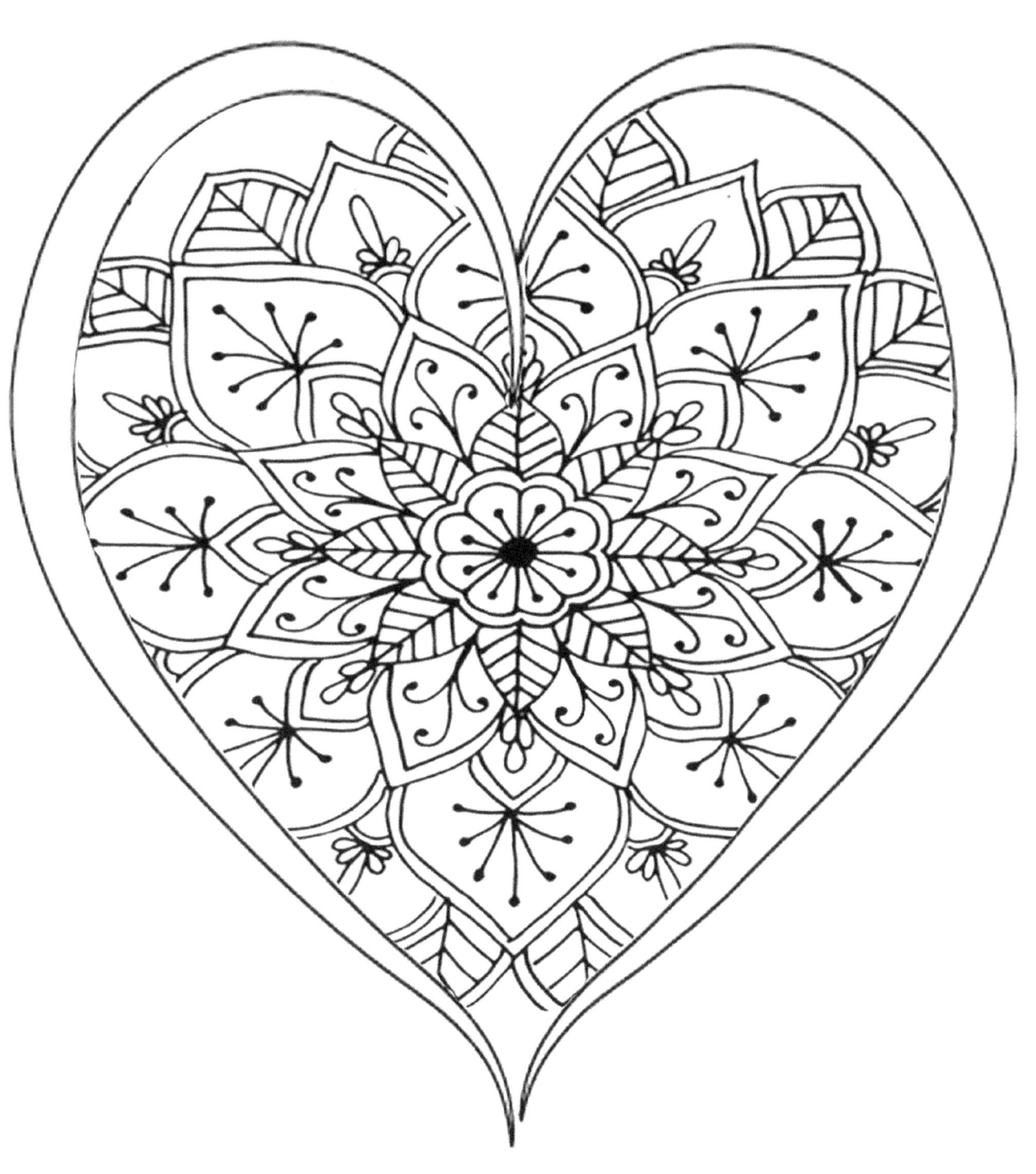

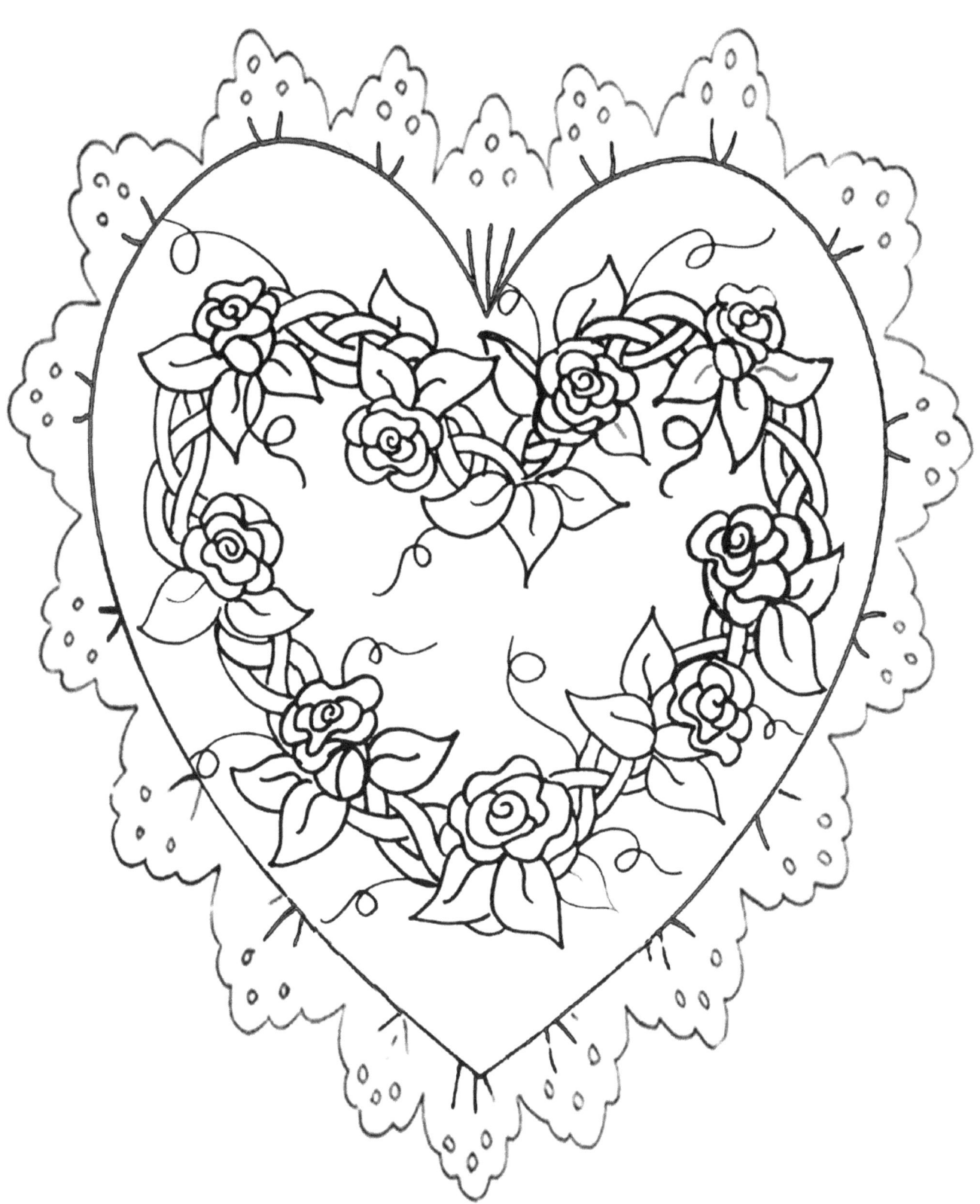

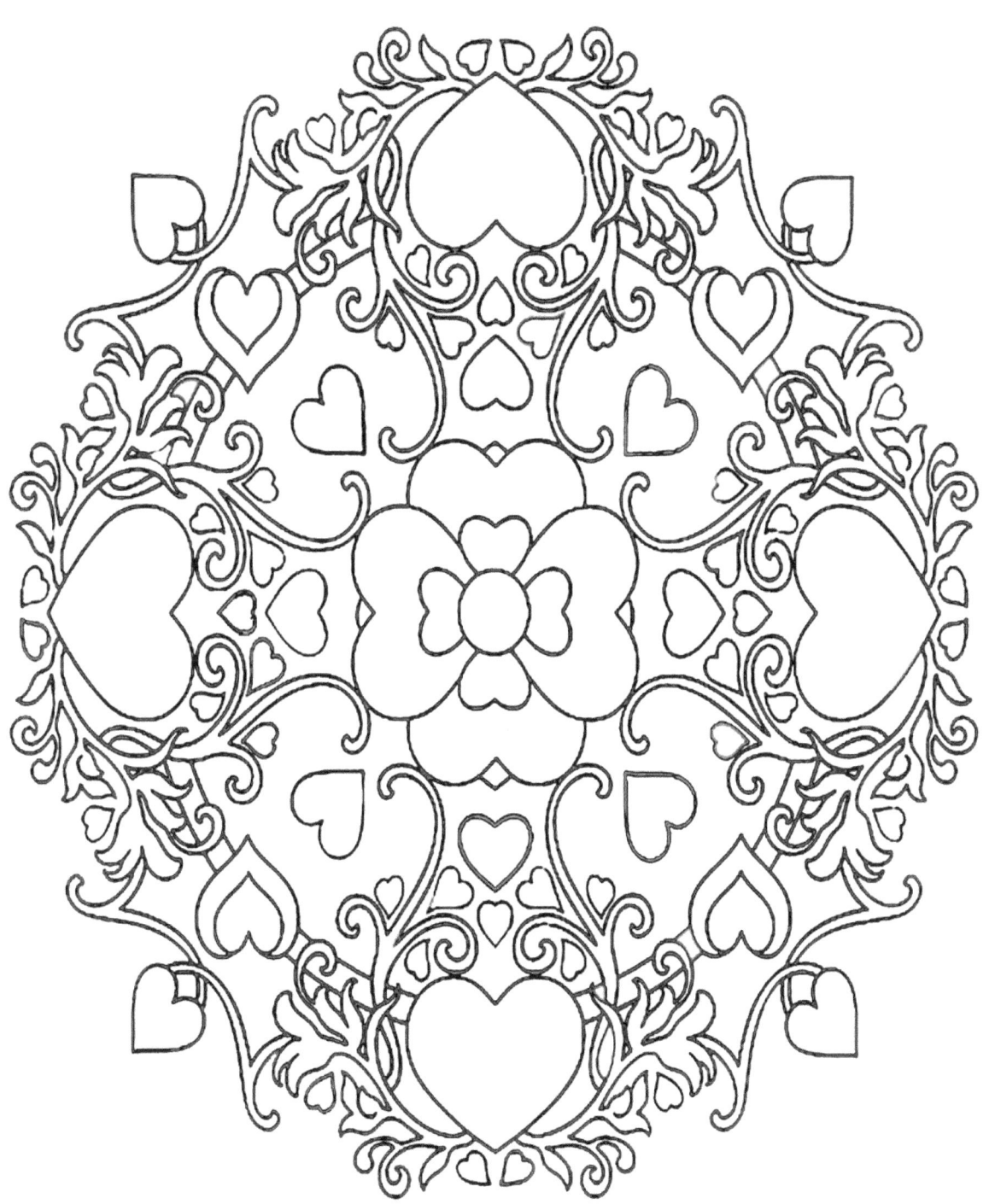

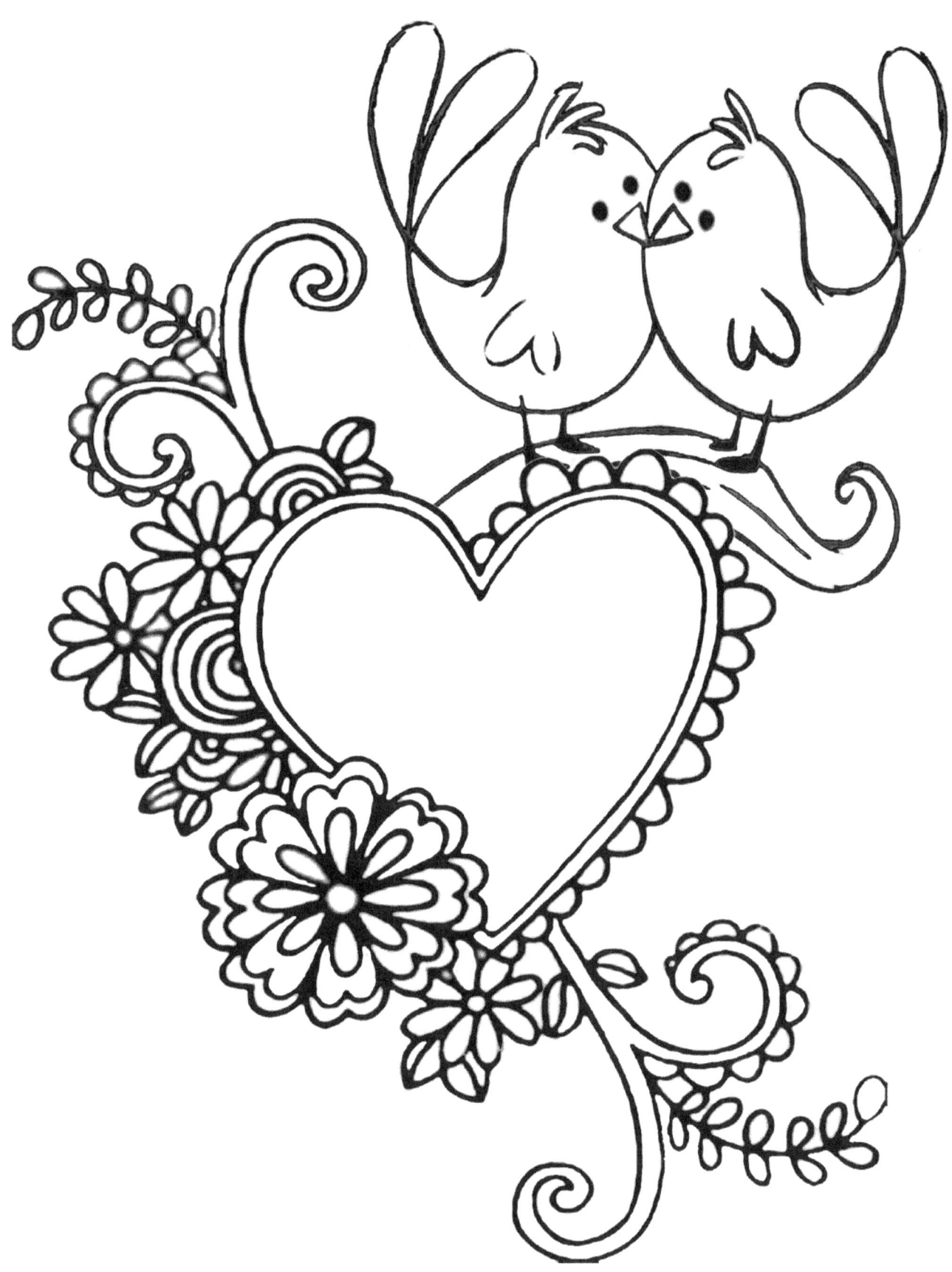

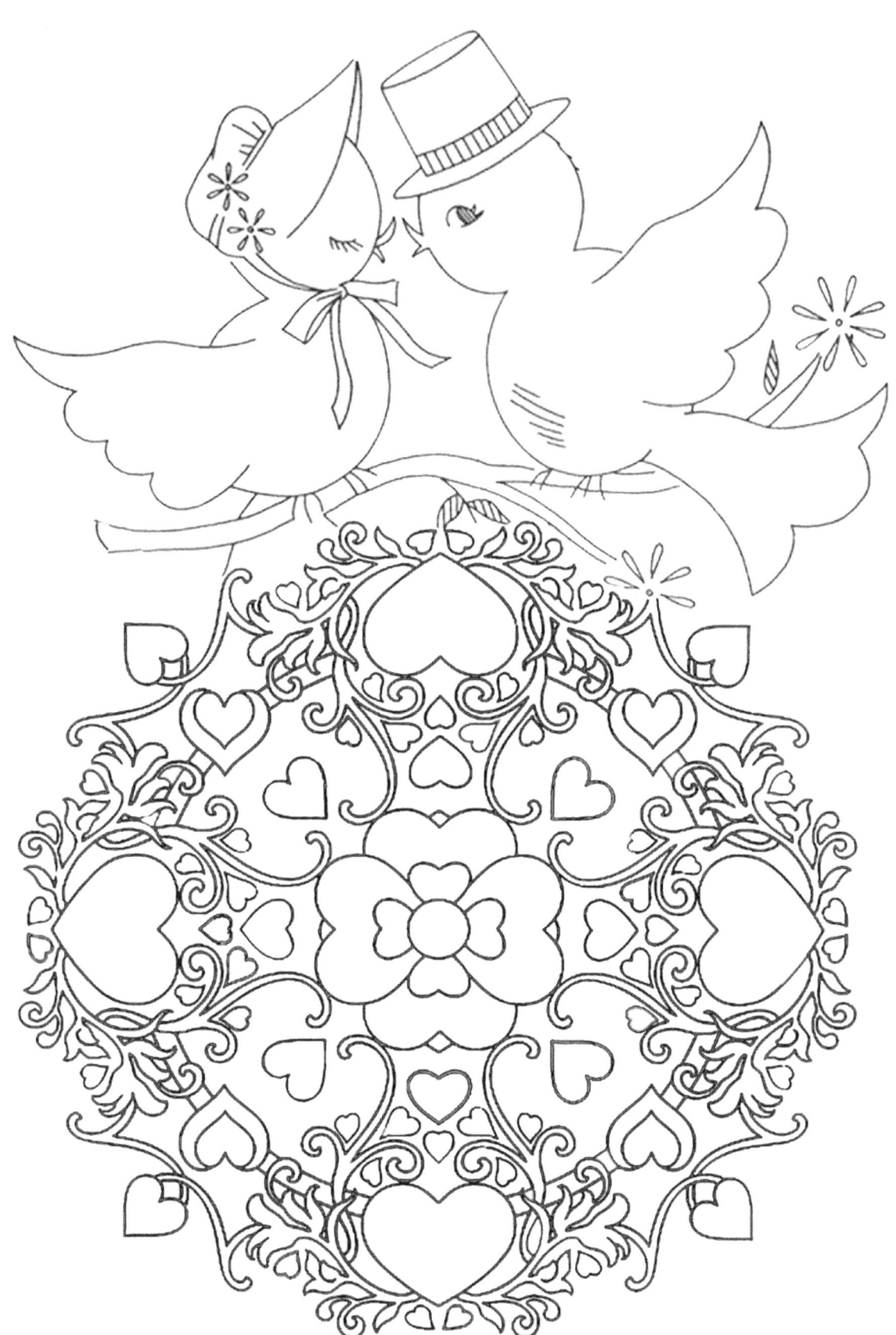

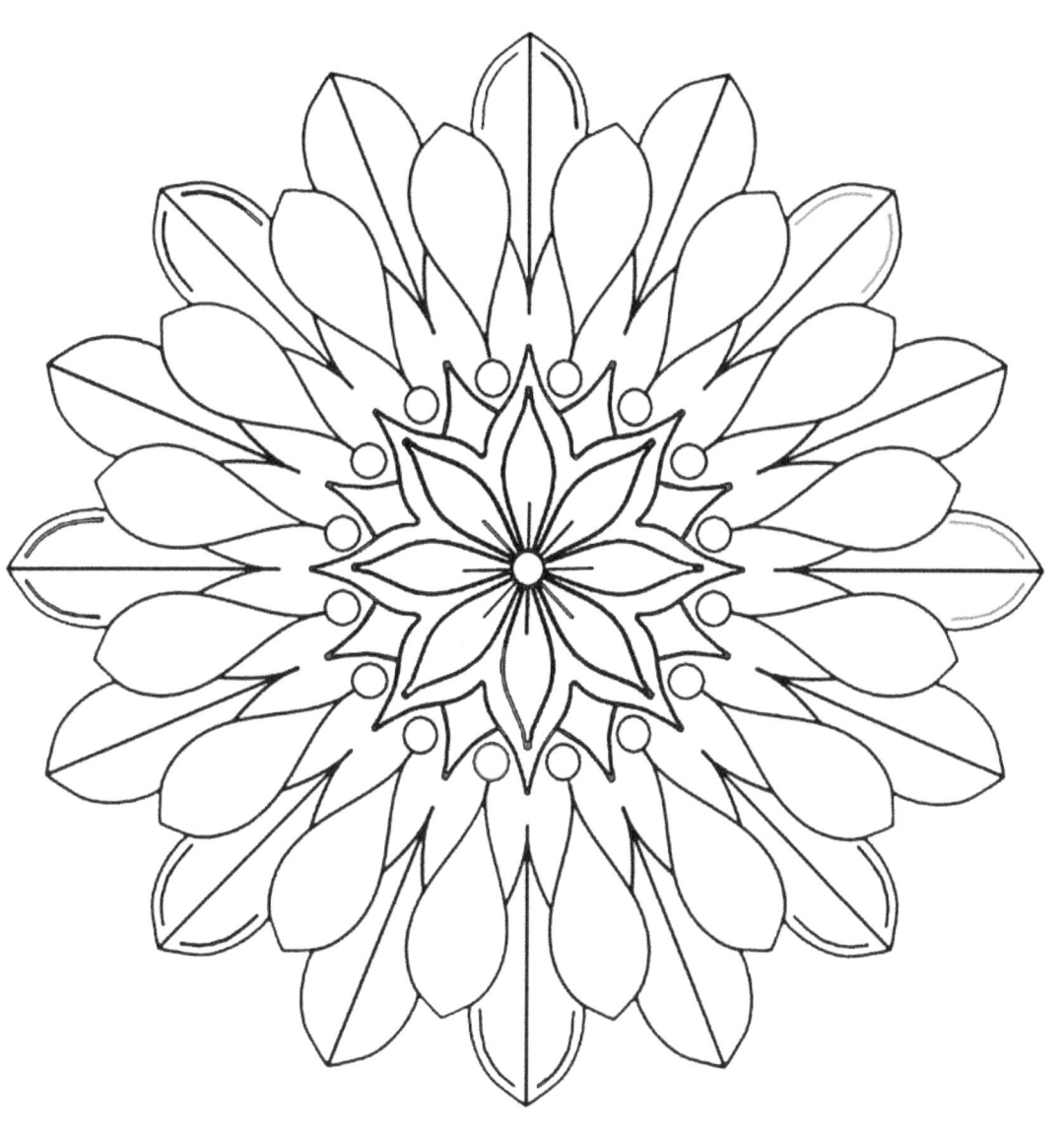

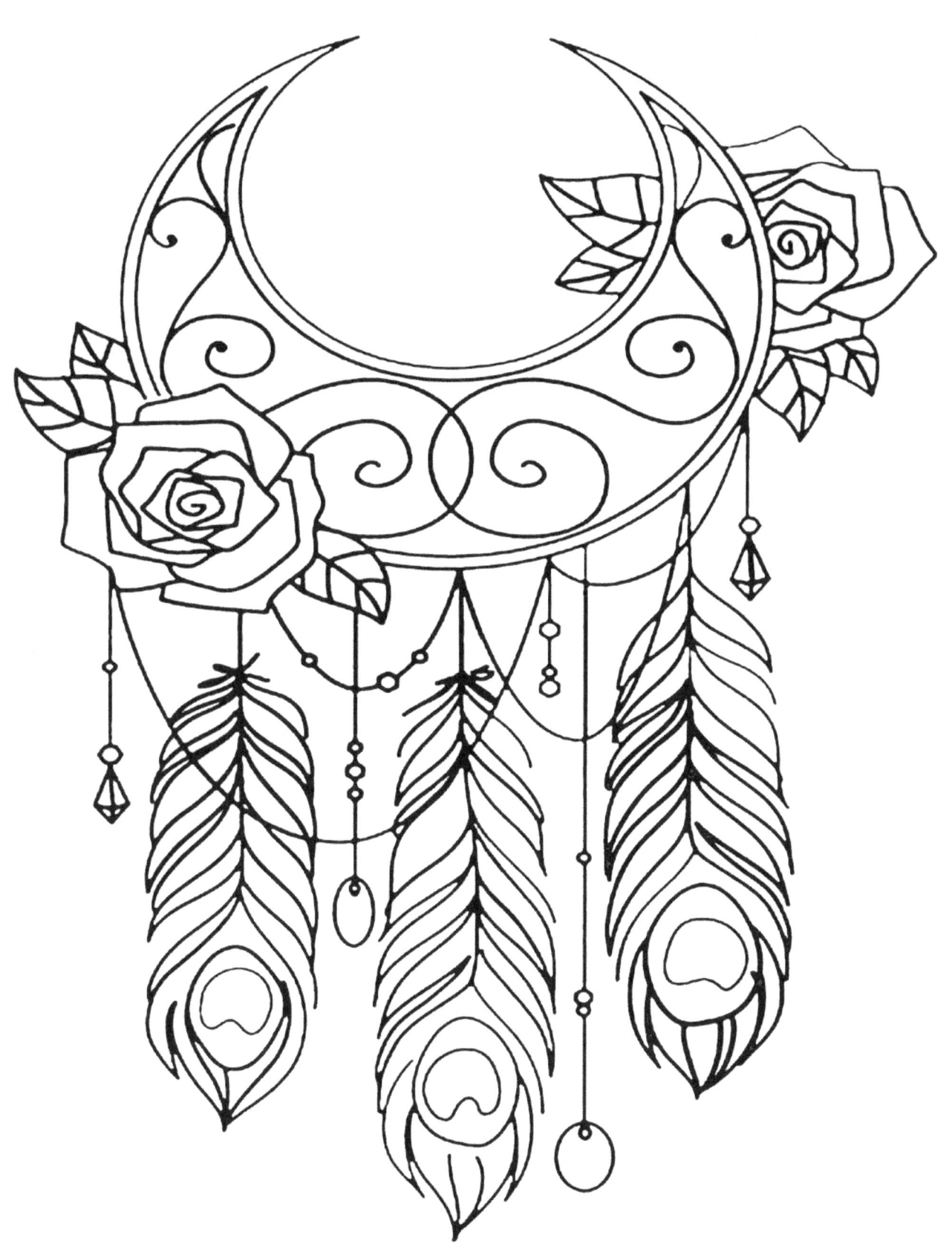

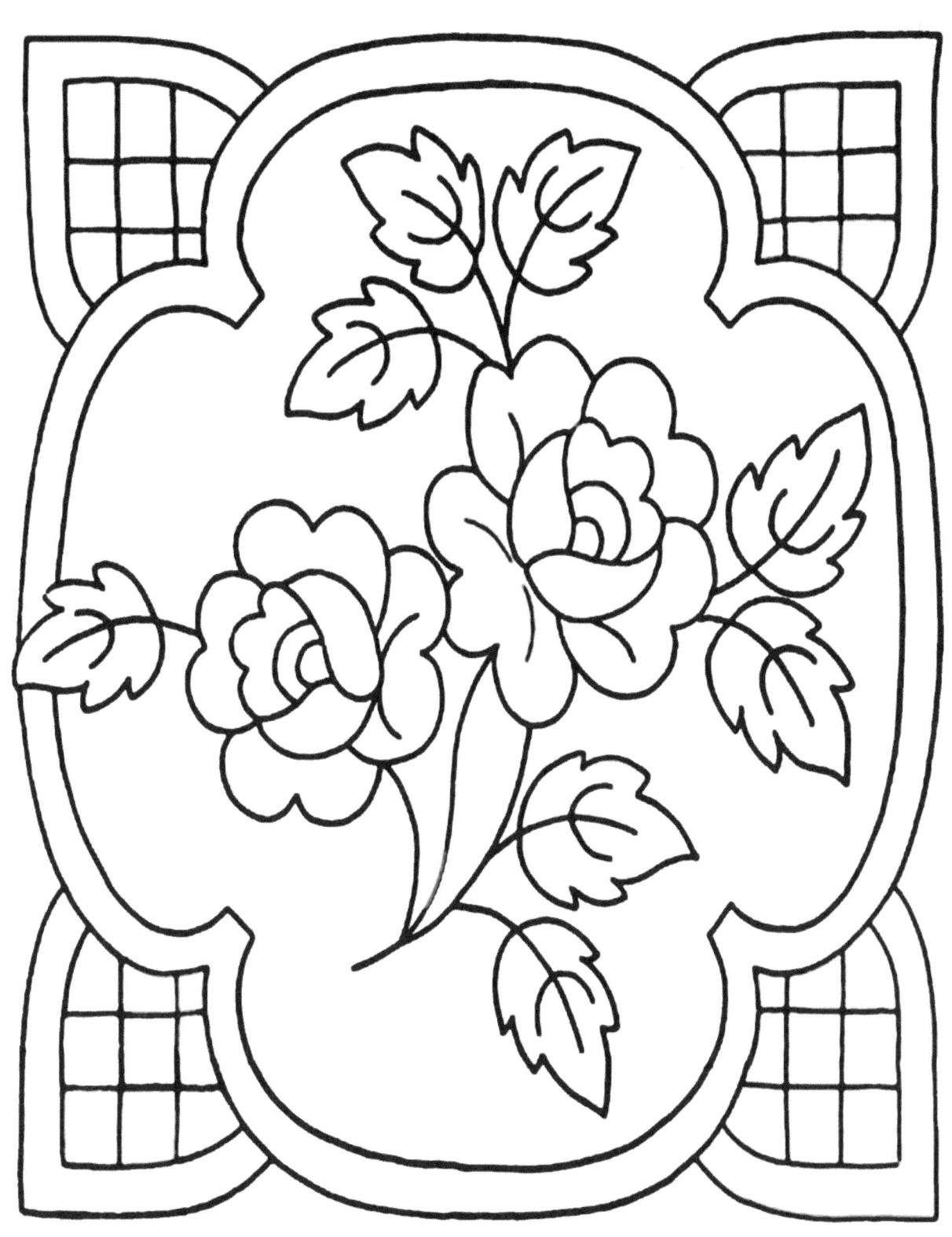

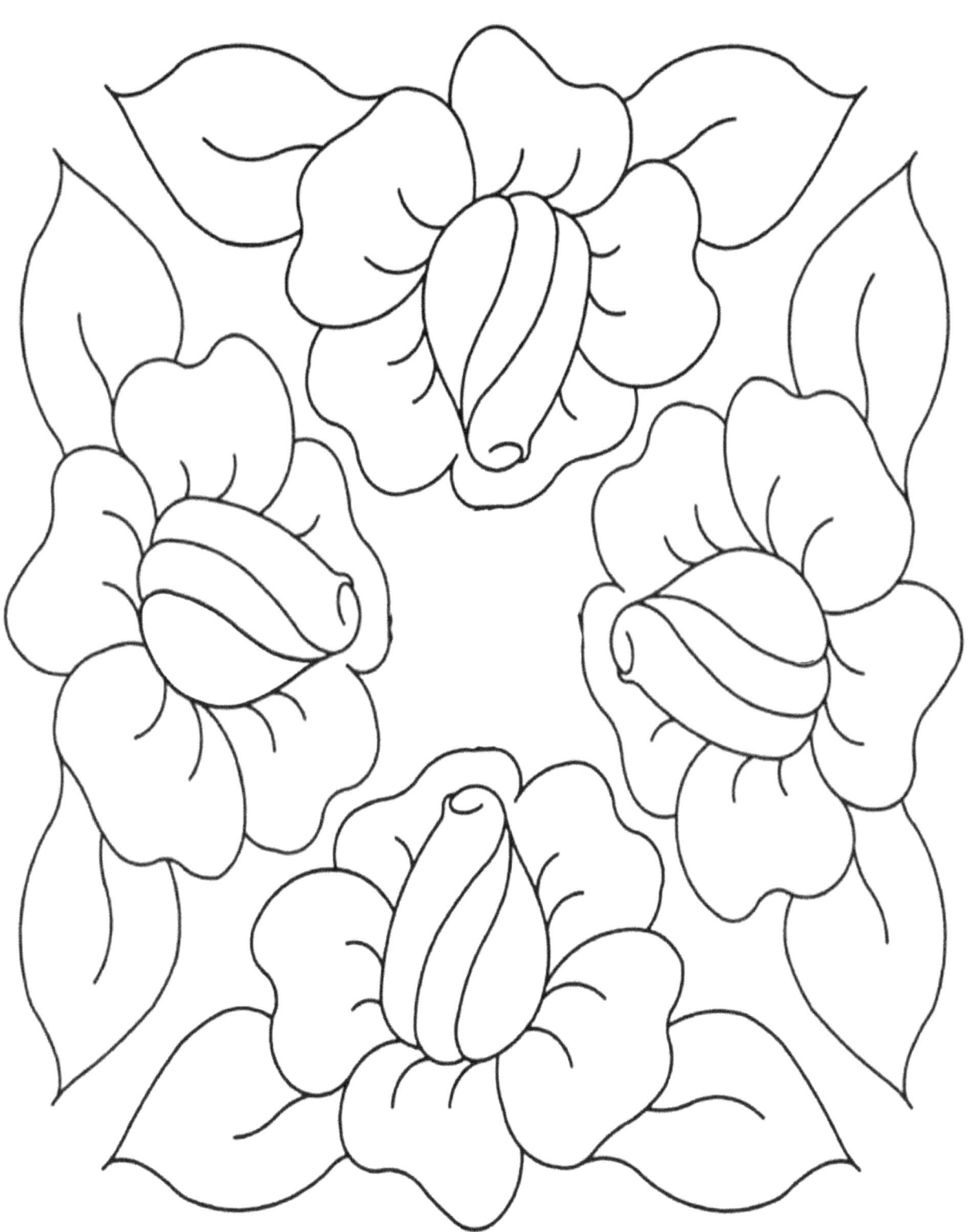

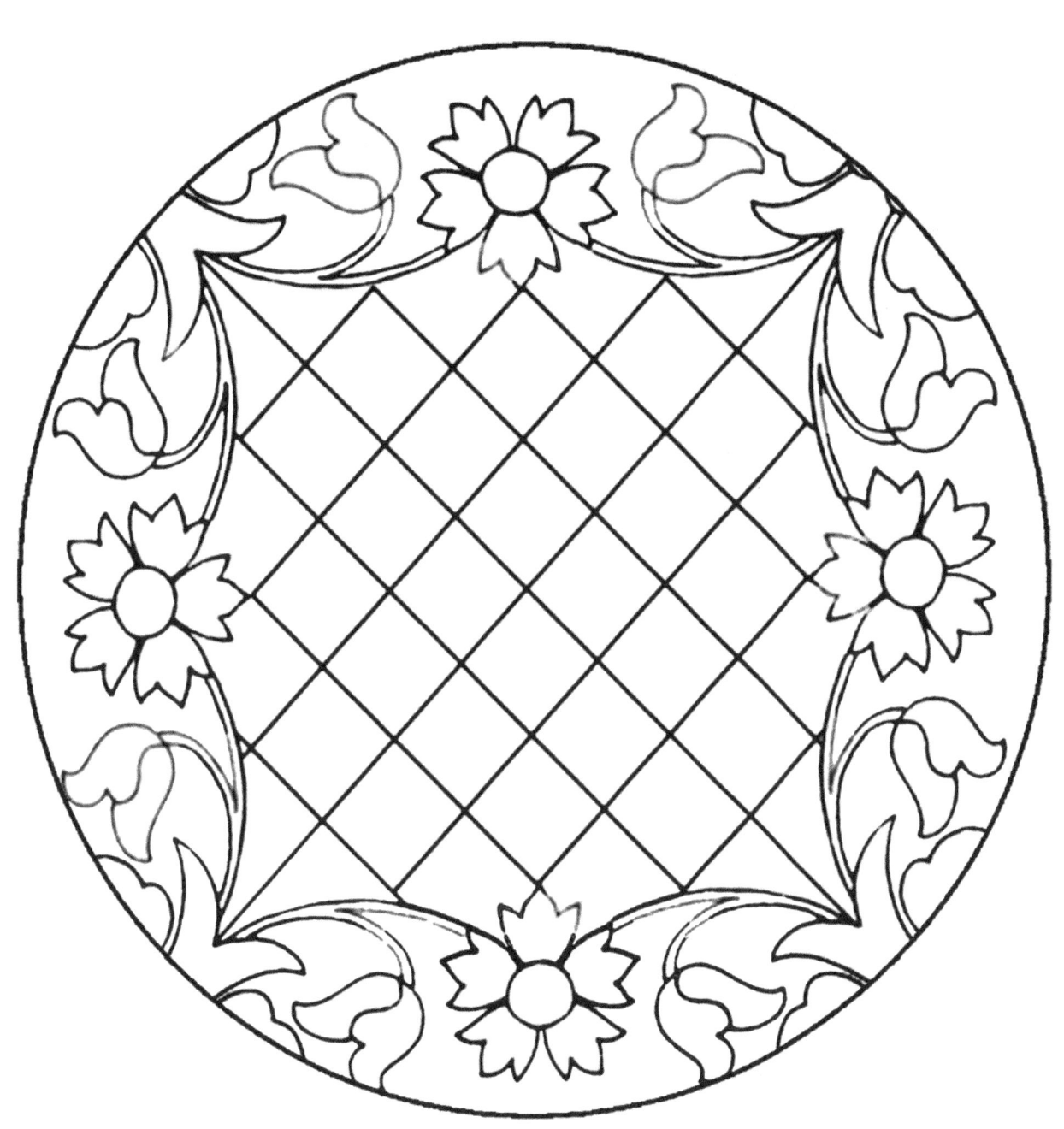

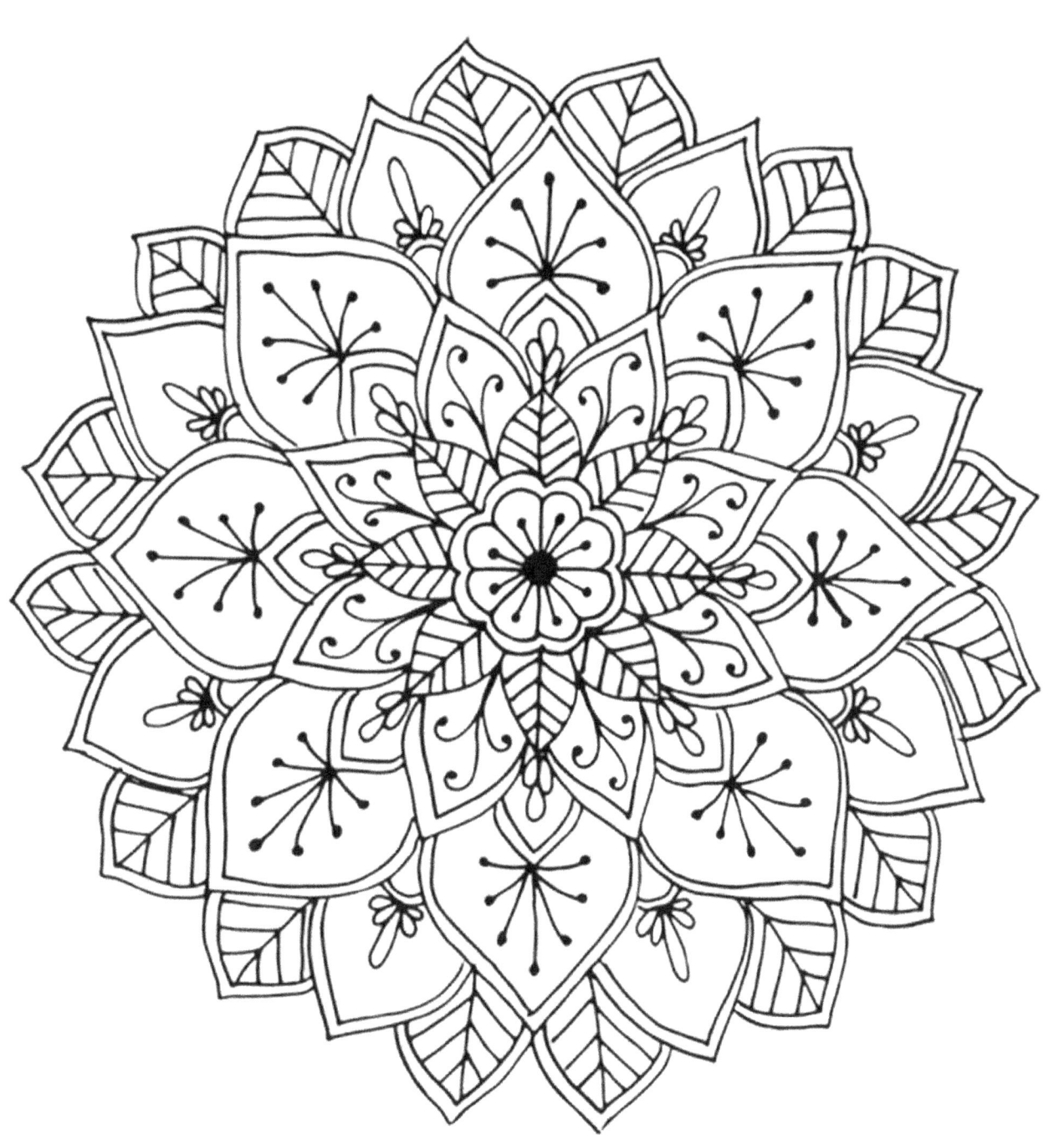

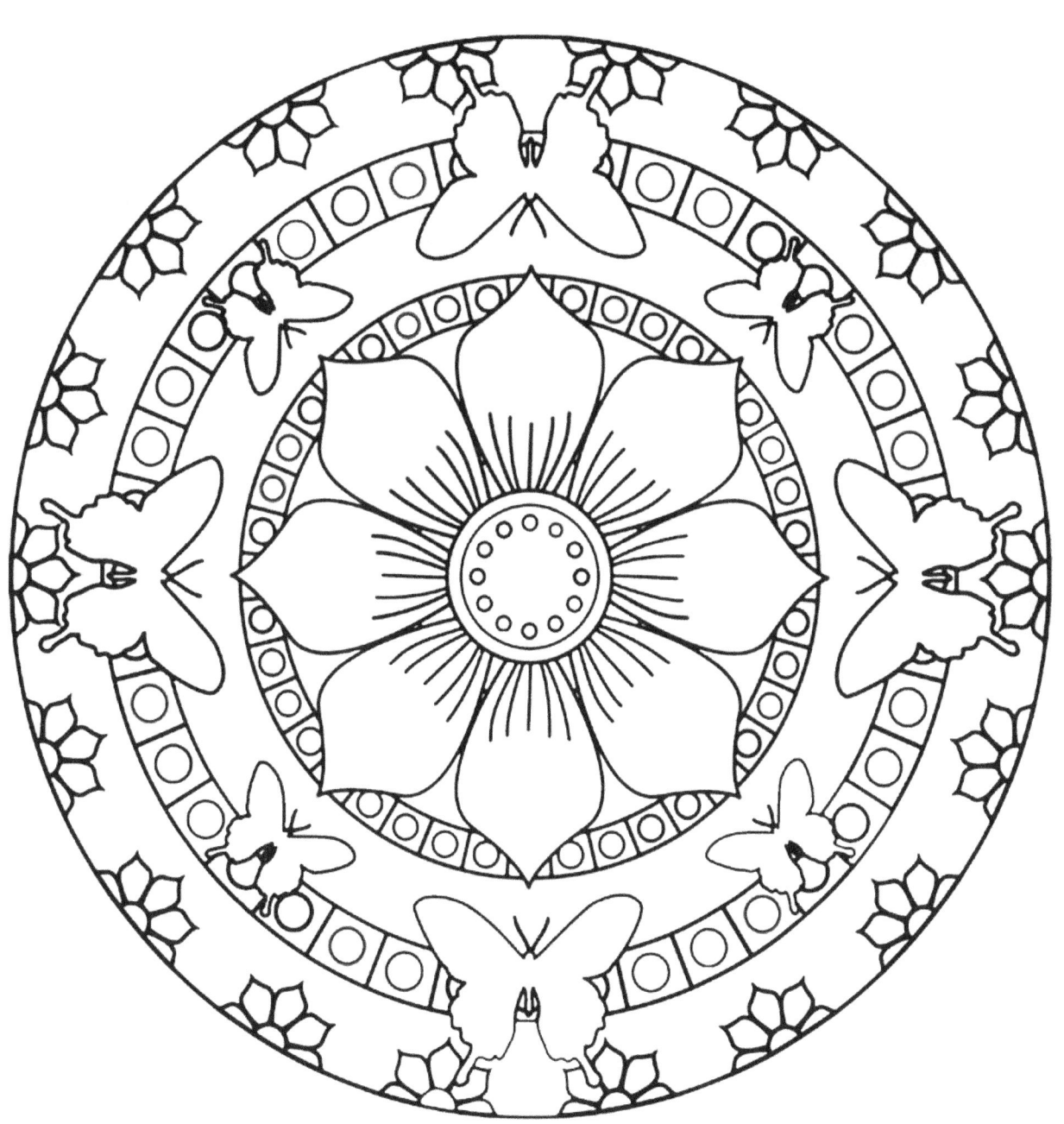

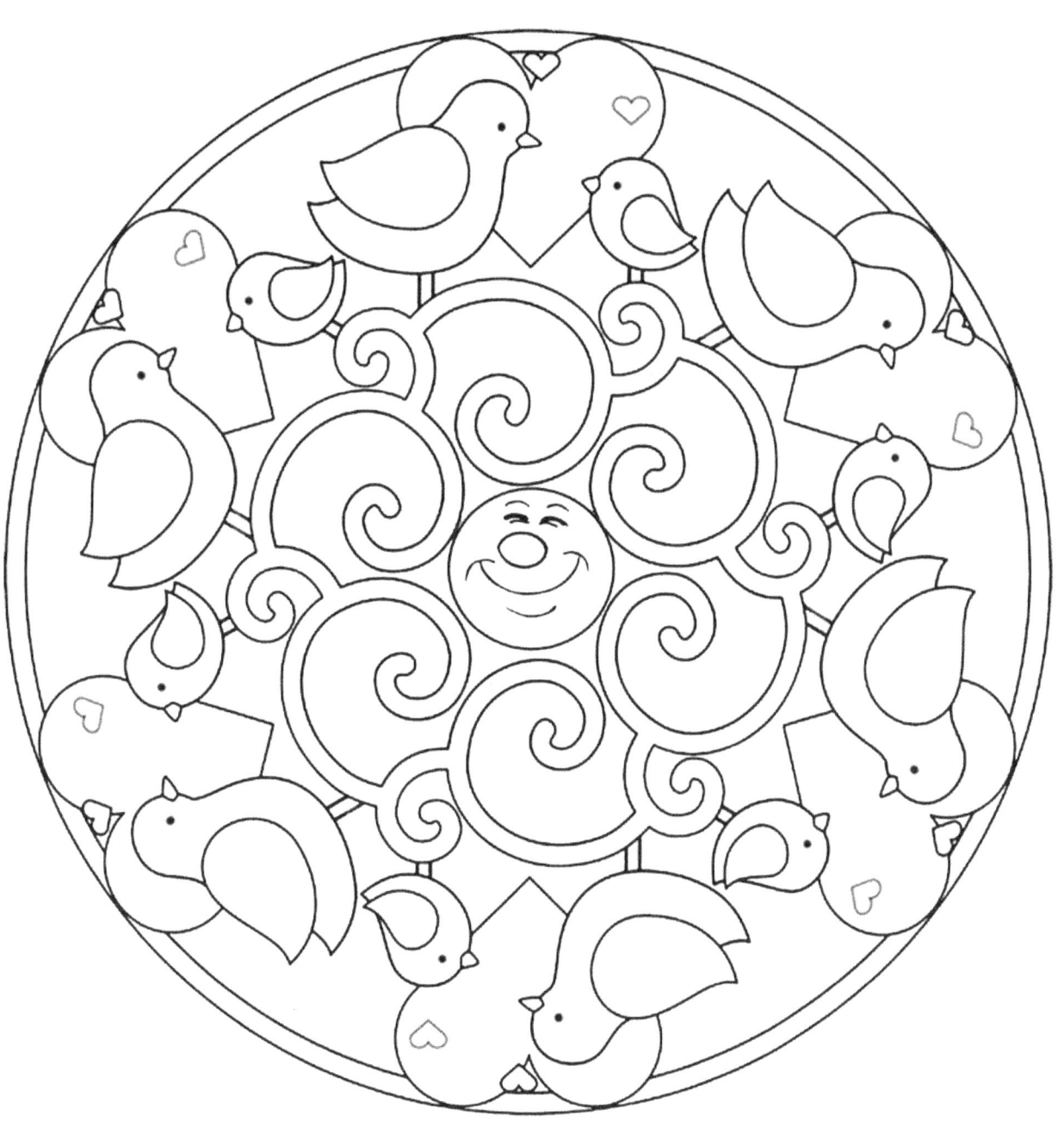

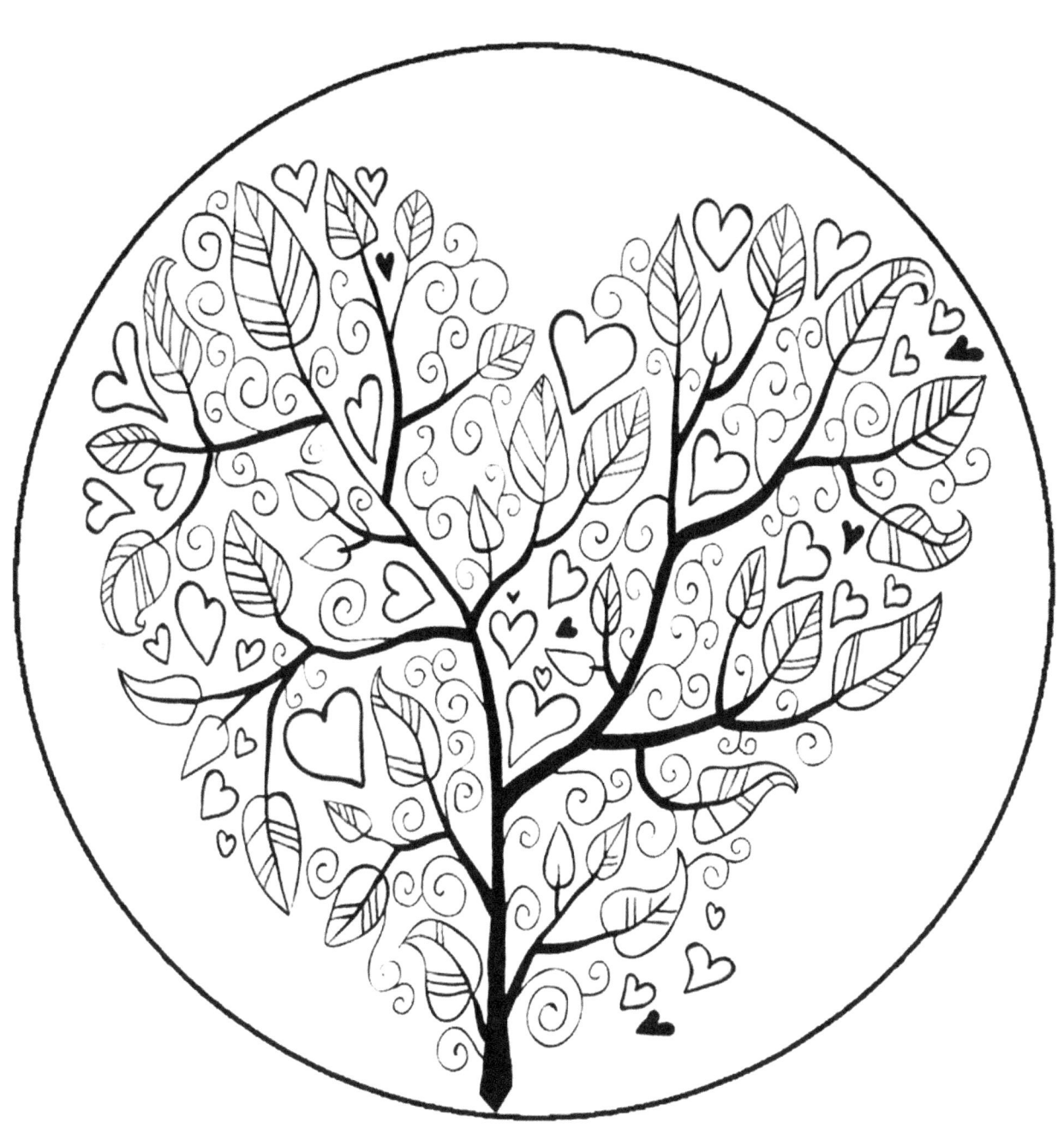

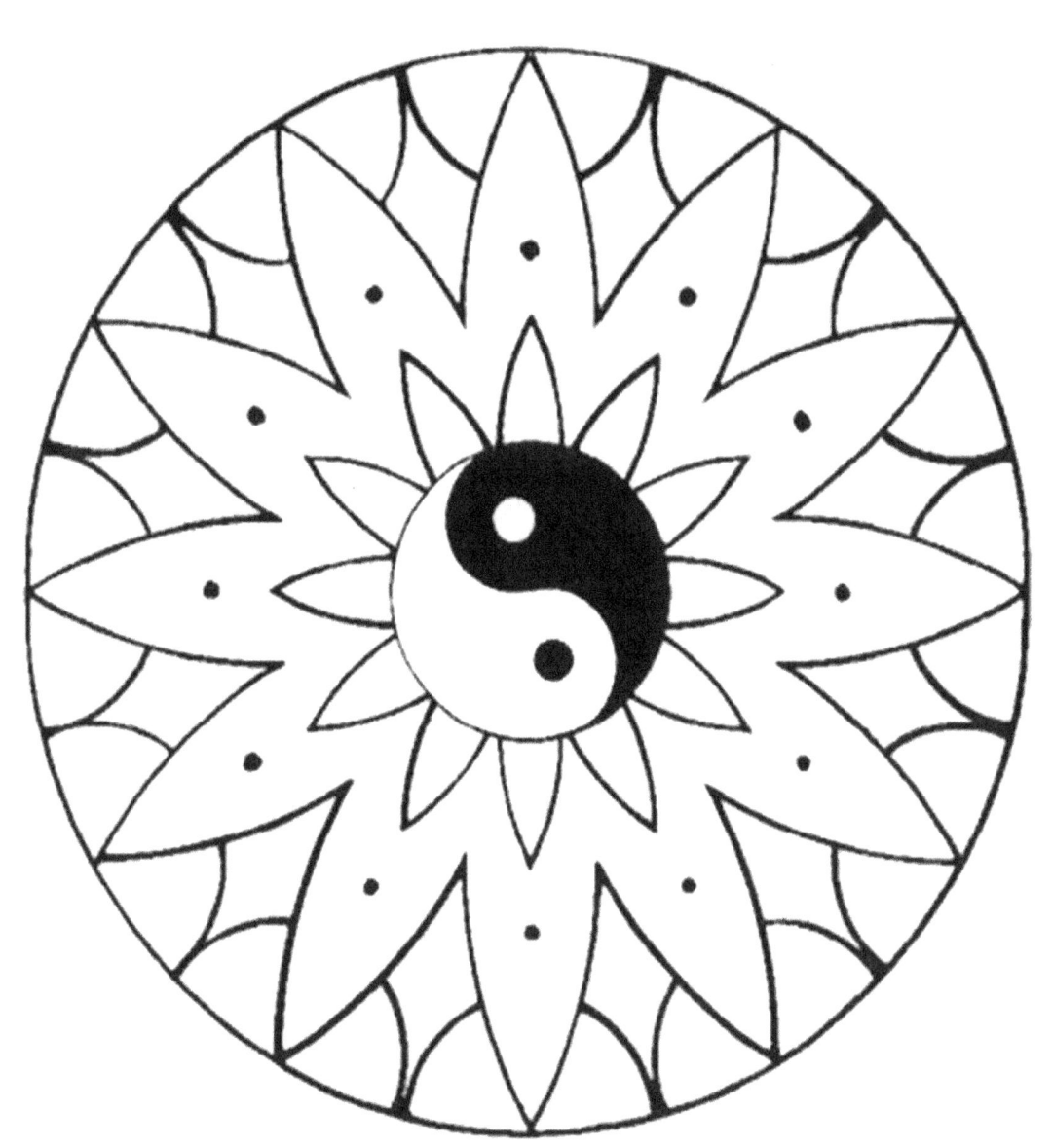

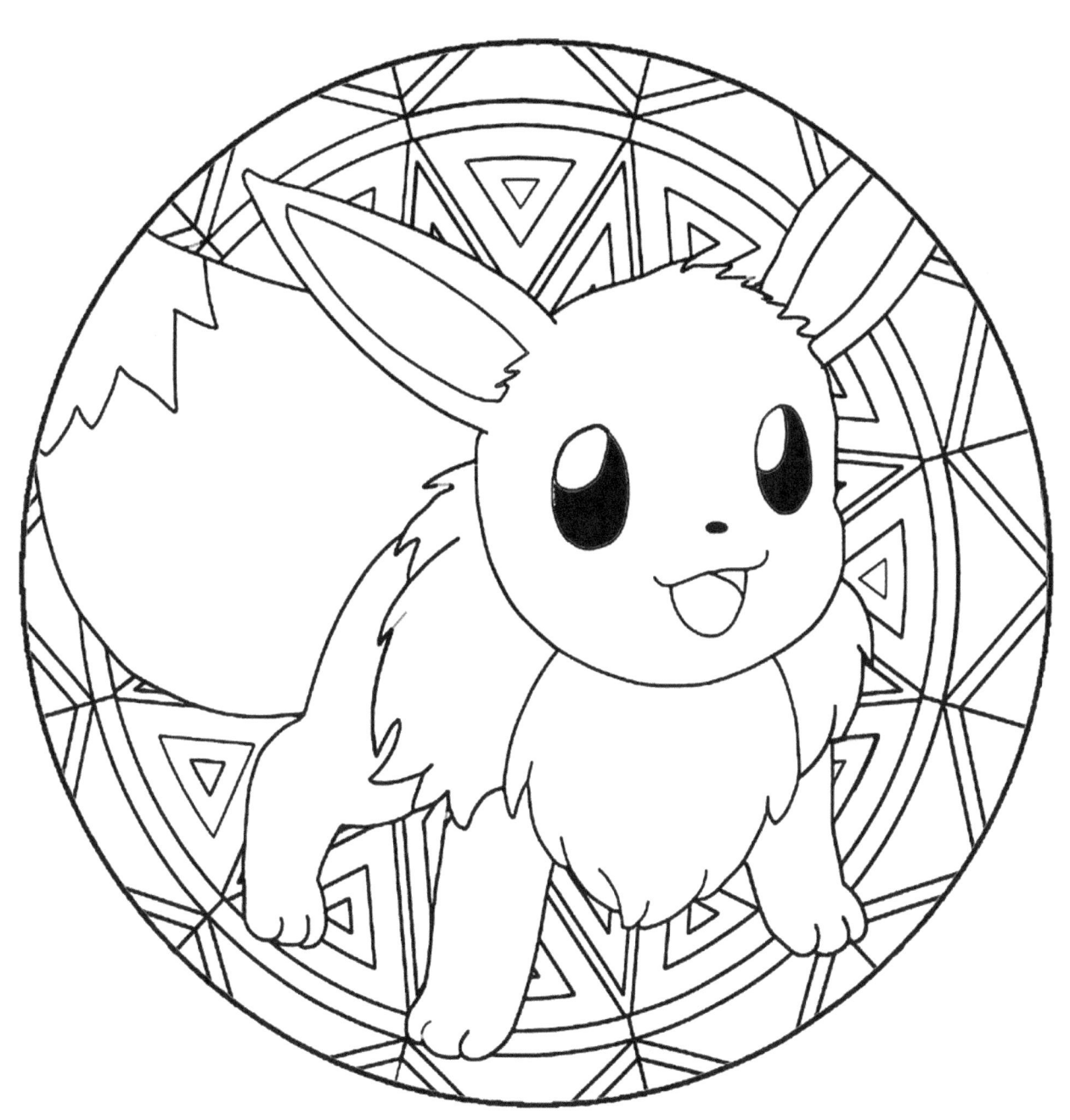

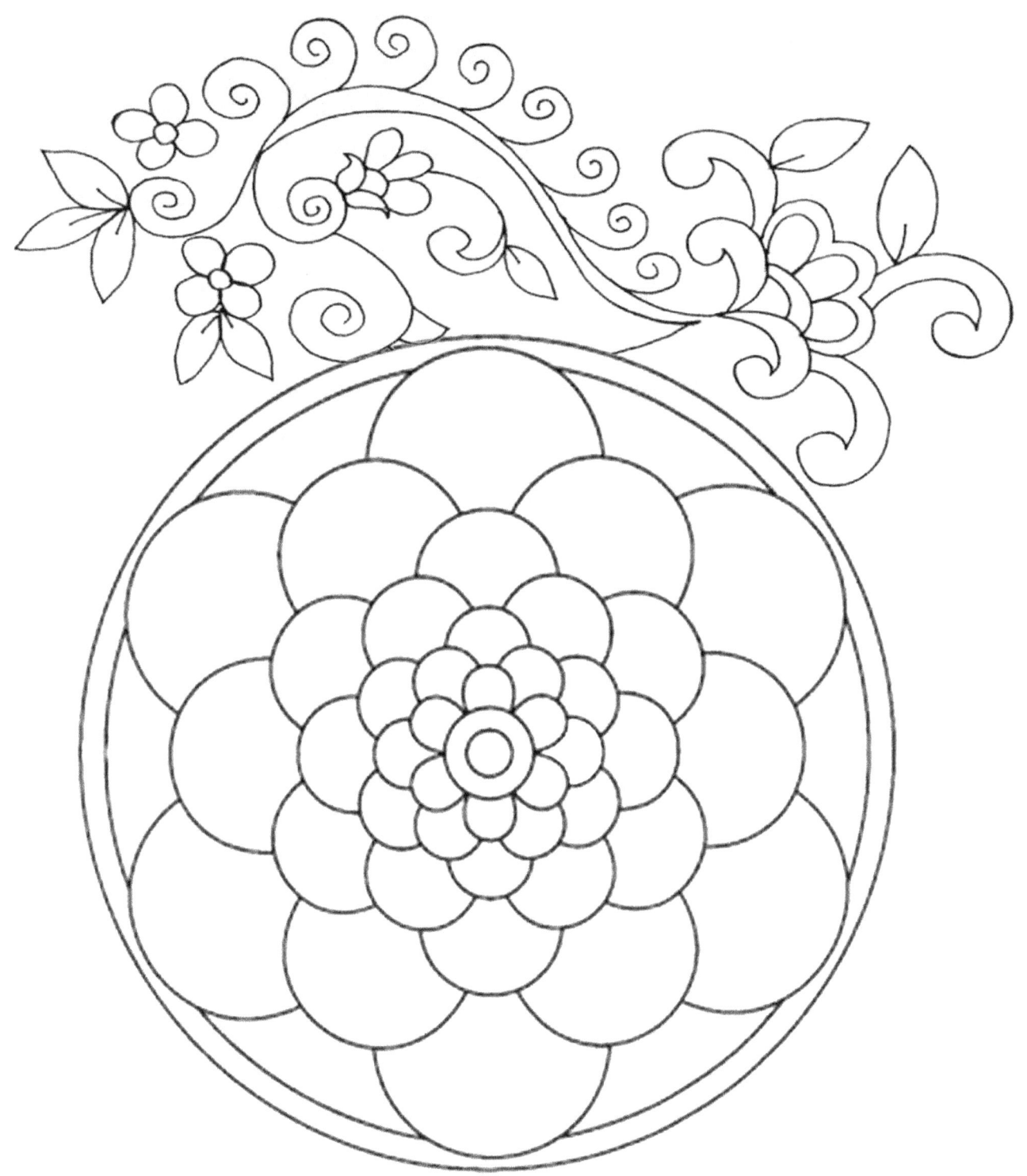

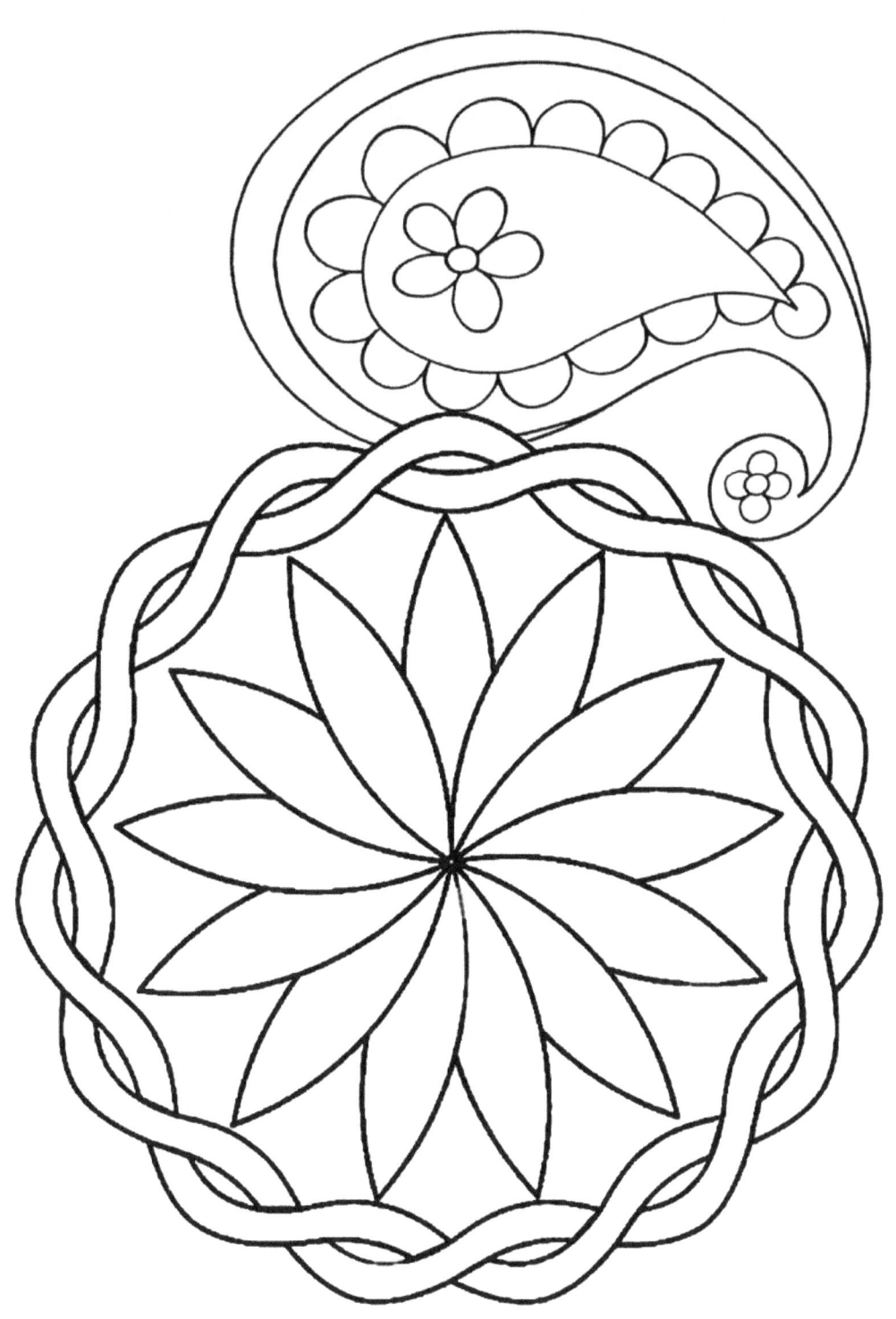

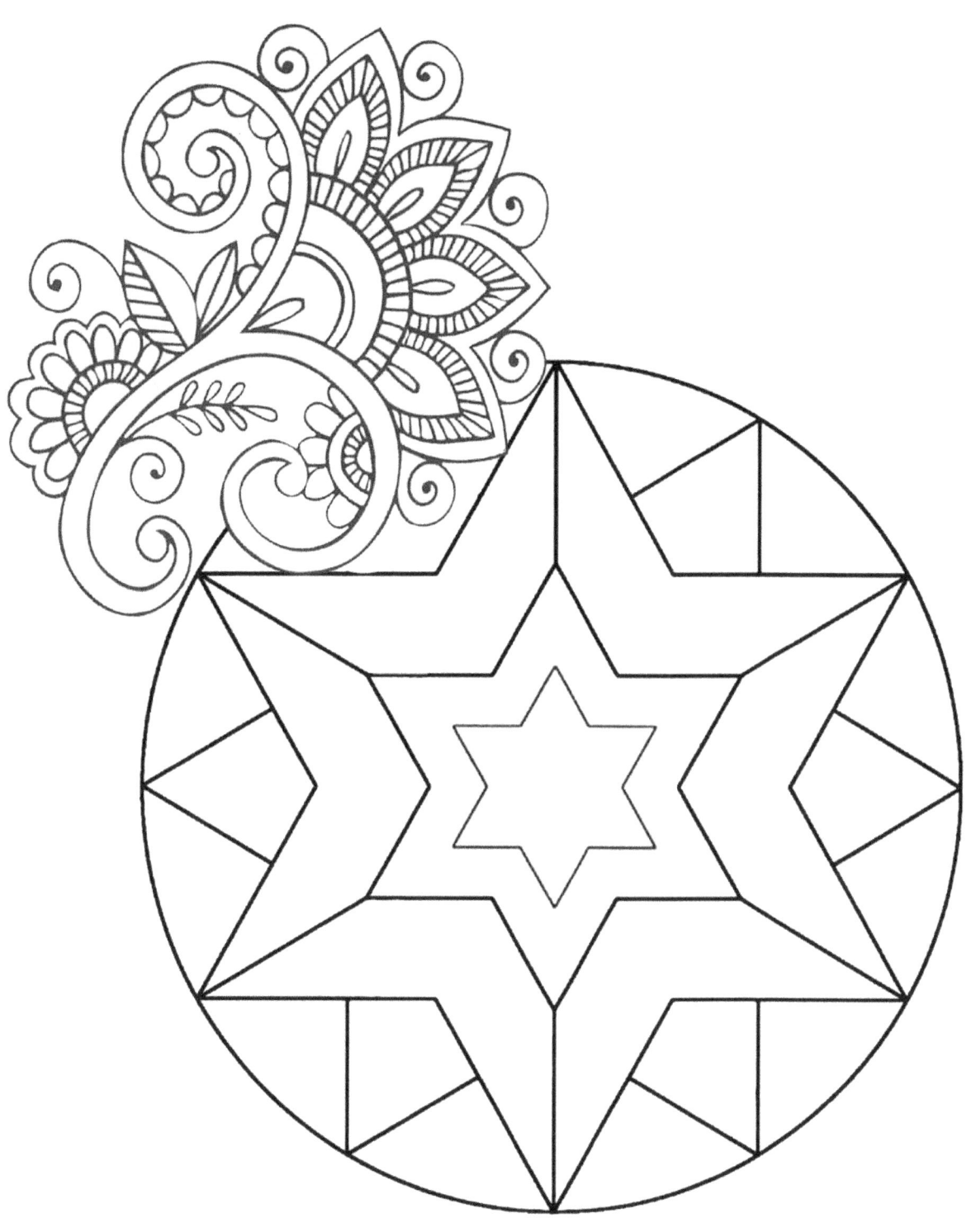

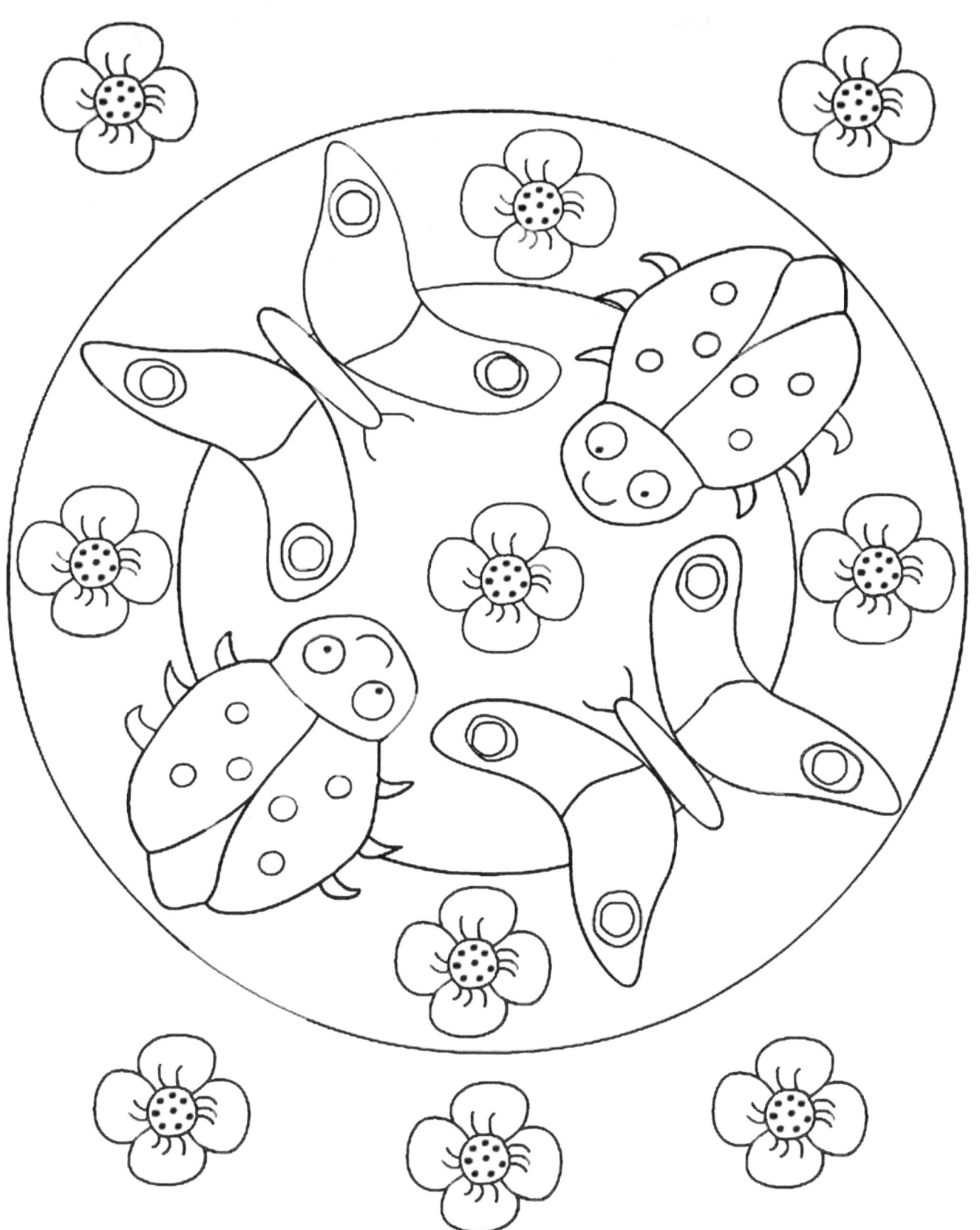

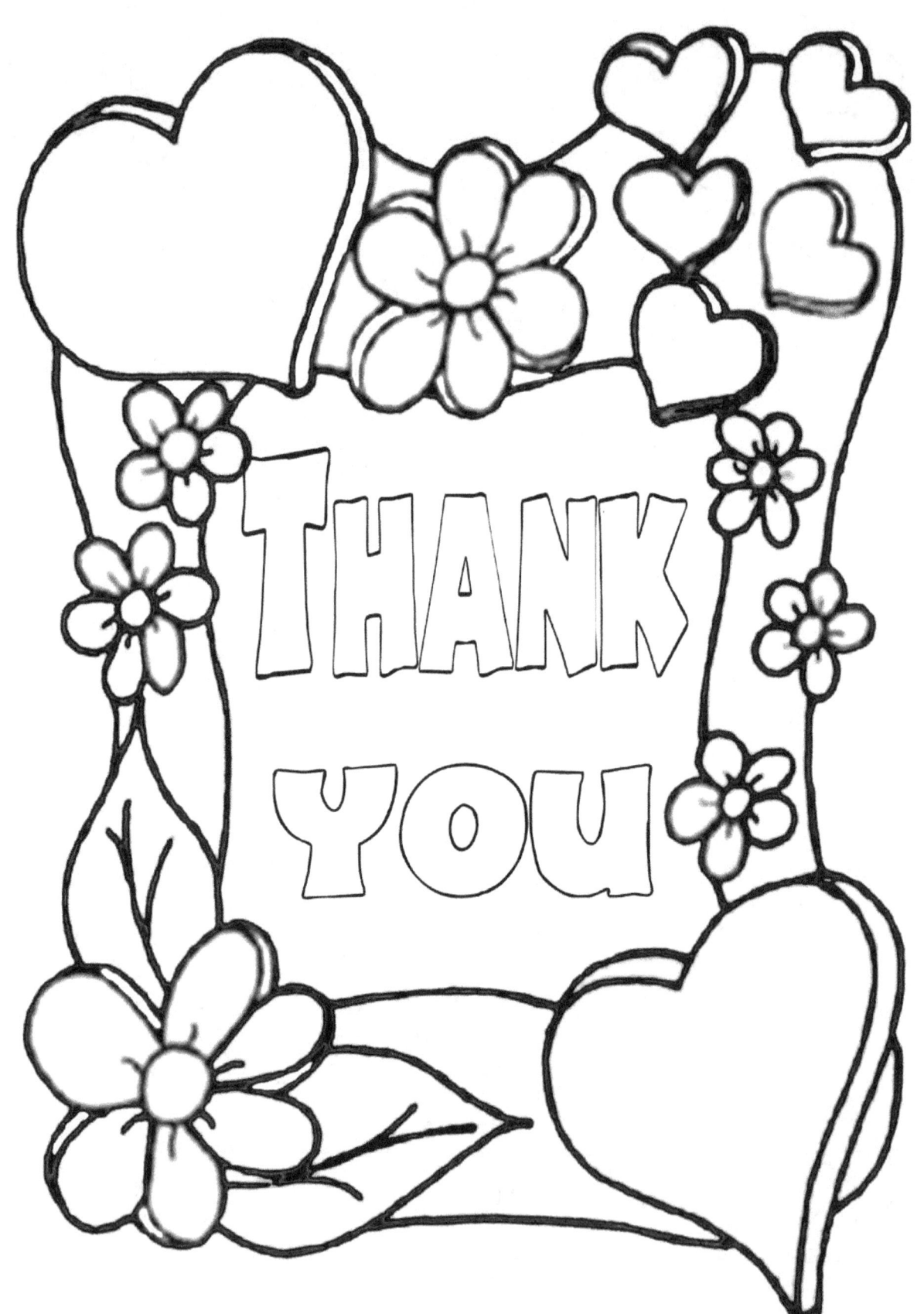